THE PEACE OF GOD

PHILIPPIANS 4:6-7

BY A. S. PAUL

CONTENT

3. OBJECTIVES
4. DEFINITIONS OF PEACE
5. KINDS OF PEACE
6. WHAT THIS PEACE DOES
7. THE NECESSITY OF PEACE
8. SCRIPTURAL FACTS ABOUT PEACE
9. THE DEMANDS FOR EXPERIENCING THE PEACE OF GOD
10. THINGS TO DO TO HAVE THE PEACE OF GOD
11. THINGS THAT HINDER PEACE
12. NOTE
13. COUNCIL

UNLESS OTHERWISE STATED, ALL SCRIPTURE QUOTATIONS ARE TAKEN FROM THE NEW KING JAMES VERSION (NKJV) OF THE HOLY BIBLE

THE PEACE OF GOD

Phil. 4:6-7

Be anxious for nothing, but in everything by prayer and supplication, with thanksgiving, let your requests be made known to God;

And **the peace of God**, which surpasses all understanding, will guard your hearts and minds through Christ Jesus.

This book is dedicated to the person of HOLY GHOST, and a fellow brother in Christ, JASPER MOTTEY

INTRODUCTION

In Christendom today, there are many controversies surrounding a Christian whether is there again THE PEACE OF GOD? Hence is proper to examine the subject THE PEACE OF GOD purely from a biblical perspective.

This is what this book seeks to do –putting it as the bible puts it.

It will, therefore, do the reader a lot of good to read with understanding and open mind. This means, you will, deliberately put aside your preconceived ideas. As you read, you will discover that, THE PEACE OF GOD is absolutely TRUTH.

This book will expose you to THE PEACE OF GOD and THE NECESSITY OF THE PEACE OF GOD and many more.

FOUR OBJECTIVES OF THIS BOOK

i. To understand THE PEACE OF GOD.
ii. To understand the necessities of THE PEACE OF GOD.

iii. To understand scriptural facts about THE PEACE OF GOD.

iv. To understand the demands for THE PEACE OF GOD.

WHAT IS PEACE?

PEACE is state or period in which there is no war or war has ended or is freedom from anxiety or distress.

BIBLICAL DEFINITIONS

PEACE is the stability of heart and mind given by God in the midst of confrontations or adversities.

2Thess. 3:16
Now may the Lord of peace Himself give you peace always

in every way. The Lord be with you all.

PEACE is a state of calmness and restfulness in the midst of pressures or urgencies.

PEACE is state of silence assurance and confidence under all circumstances.

Isa. 32:17

The work of righteousness will be peace, and the effect of righteousness, quietness and assurance forever.

KINDS OF THIS PEACE

I. **PEACE from or of God.**

This particular one is talking about the birth of our Lord JESUS CHRIST on earth.

This song explain it better.

Peace, Peace, wonderful peace,
Coming down from the Father above.
Sweep over my spirit forever, I pray,
In fathomless billows of love.

Let see something in matt. 4:16-17

16: The people who sat in darkness have seen a great light, and upon those who sat in the region and shadow of death Light has dawned.

This place the write is saying that "Jesus brings the peace of god to the people that are in distresses, pains, oppressions, etc...

17: From that time Jesus began to preach and to say, "Repent, for the kingdom of heaven is at hand."

In this case Jesus is telling the world that we should come closer to God for he has come with

the peace of god. Thus to say to reconcile us to God the father.

To prove this well, let see Matt. 10

13: If the household is worthy, let your peace come upon it. But if it is not worthy, let your peace return to you.

This means that: when you send the gospel of PEACE or reconciliation or repentance to someone, and the person accept it then, that particular person has received PEACE

that we are talking about. But if not the person has no PEACE

ii. **PEACE with God This is the finishing work of Christ Jesus on earth. Thus to say:**

- **His doctrines**
- **His fellowship**
- **His suffering**
- **His crucifixion**
- **His death**
- **His resurrection**

- **His ascension**

See this: phil. 3

10: that I may *know Him*
and the power of *His
resurrection,* and the
fellowship of *His
sufferings*, being
conformed to *His death*,

In this case, to know him means:

1. **His doctrines, thus, to know who Christ is and his teaching**
2. **His fellowship, when one knows Christ and his teachings it very easy for that man**

to fellowship with
the father.

WHAT THIS PEACE DOES.

1. **THE PEACE OF GOD will keep you from all worries and anxiety.**
2. **THE PEACE OF GOD will keep you from depression and tensions.**
3. **THE PEACE OF GOD will**

separate you from the world.

4. No matter the circumstances of the world THE PEACE OF GOD is assured.
5. THE PEACE OF GOD saves one from destructions of life.
6. THE PEACE OF GOD liberates one from the fear of this world.

7. **THE PEACE OF GOD makes people great beyond their imagination.**
8. **THE PEACE OF GOD brings peace to the world.**
9. **THE PEACE OF GOD makes one to live in peace with all.**

THE NECESSITY OF PEACE

1. The peace of God is needed to withstand and overcome the regular pressures and troubles of this world.

John 16

33: These things I have spoken to you, that in Me you may have peace. In the world you will have tribulation; but be of good cheer, I have overcome the world."

This simply means that in Christ, a Christian or a believer has THE PEACE OF GOD.

- Jesus has conquered the world for us to have this PEACE we are talking about.
- This PEACE that we are talking about is not outside of CHRIST, because

he said “in ME you may have PEACE”

- The only mandate here, is for us to accept Christ as our Lord and personal savior to be able to have this PEACE OF GOD.

2. The peace of God is needed to confront and conquer sudden storms that may arise through life.

Mark 4

35: On the same day, when
evening had come, He said to
them, "Let us cross over to the
other side."
36: Now when they had left the
multitude, they took Him along
in the boat as He was. And
other little boats were also with
Him.
37: And a great windstorm
arose, and the waves beat into
the boat, so that it was already
filling.
38: But He was in the stern,
asleep on a pillow. And they
awoke Him and said to Him,
"Teacher, do You not care that
we are perishing?"
39: Then He arose and rebuked
the wind, and said to the sea,
"*Peace*, be still!" And the wind

ceased and there was a great calm.

- **This place, Christ is confronting the sudden storms of life that wanted to stop His ministry.**
- **Remember that storm arises suddenly, and Christ rebuked the storm with THE PEACE OF GOD that he has within himself.**

- Remember that when Christ used THE PEACE OF GOD to rebuked the storm, it has stopped

3. The peace of God is needed for the workings of God.

- In Gen. 2:21 GOD needs total silence for his work to be done, and that silence is equal to THE PEACE that we are talking about here. GOD caused the man (Adam) to sleep deep for the Lord to have PEACE to do his work, other than that, Adam would have caused trouble.

- In Acts 12:6-8, GOD needs PEACE to liberate his martyr from

the prison of the wicked one. That why, when all were asleep the angel of the Lord came to saved Peter.

4. **The peace of God is needed to receive instruction, revelation and direction from God. Ps. 46**

10: *Be still*, and know that I am God; I will be exalted

among the nations, I will be exalted in the earth!

- **BE STILL there means have THE PEACE.**
- **When you have PEACE, you give God opportunity to take over and direct you in all that you are doing.**
- **And the Lord will show you who He is, above your imaginations.**

5. **The peace of God is the fountain for true joy. Prov. 12**

20: Deceit is in the heart of those who devise evil, But counselors of *peace* have joy.

- **You can see from this scripture that, THE PEACE OF GOD gives joy.**
- **If you are the one that promote PEACE will have**

the true joy, thus everlasting joy.

- **Now let us see something from Rom. 15**

  13: Now may the God of hope fill you with all joy and *peace* in believing, that you may abound in hope by the power of the Holy Spirit.

- **This place the writer is saying that, God will fill us with JOY and PEACE**

- So therefore, you can see clearly that THE PEACE OF GOD gives us joy.

SCRIPTURAL FACTS ABOUT PEACE

1. God is the God of peace

Rom. 15:33; 16:20; 1Cor. 14:33;

1Thess. 5:23; Heb. 13:20

2. Peace is a blessing and provision of God

for His people. Ps. 29:11;

Isa. 26:12; Rom. 14:17

3. The covenant of peace connects people to God. Isa. 54:10; Ezek. 34:25; 37:26; Mal. 2:4-5; 1Pet. 2:9

Note: please read all the above scripture it will help you to understand well THE PEACE that we are talking about.

THE DEMANDS FOR EXPERIENCING THE PEACE OF GOD. (ROM. 14:19)

1. **The demand for experiencing the peace of God is by Justification by faith – Rom. 5:1**

2. The demand for experiencing the peace of God is by the heart and mind that stayed on God. Isa. 26:3; John 14:27

3. The demand for experiencing the peace of God is by handing over cares and worries to God.

Phil. 4:7

4. The demand for experiencing the peace of God is by intimacy with God – Job 22:21

5. The demand for experiencing the peace of God is by hearkening to His Word and Commandment.

Ps. 119:165

6. The demand for experiencing the peace of God is by access to the voice of God. Ps. 23:1-2; 85:8; John 16:33

7. The demand for experiencing the peace of God is by walking in wisdom. 1Kgs.

5:12-; Prov. 3:13-17; Jam. 3:17

8. The demand for experiencing the peace of God is by the working of the spirit – Rom. 14:17; Gal. 5:22; Rom. 8:6

9. The demand for experiencing the peace of God is by walking in

meekness and humility.

Ps. 37:11; Matt. 11:29; Phil. 4:9

10. The demand for experiencing the peace of God is by walking in love and unity – Eph. 4:1-3; Col. 3:14-15

11. The demand for experiencing the peace of God is by walking in goodness and peacefulness

2Kgs. 9:22-24; Isa. 57:21; Isa. 48:18-22;

Rom. 2:8-10; Jam. 3:17-18

12. The demand for experiencing the peace of God is by walking in righteousness and the fear of God.

Ps. 37:37; 85:10

THINGS TO DO TO HAVE THE PEACE OF GOD.

1. Accept Christ as Lord and personal savior of your life. Joh.3:16,

- Believe that Christ is the son of God.

- **To confess your sins to God to forgive you your sins.**
- **Accept him as the manager of your affairs.**

2. **If you get worry you can have this PEACE, so forget all your worries or put all your worries at the feet of Christ.**

3. Give yourself continually to the word of God and prayer. Acts 6:4
4. Make sure you have PEACE with others.
5. Let your heart be at PEACE always.
6. Never encouraged self-pity. Num.9:8 Isa. 55:12

7. **Trust in the Lord always.**
8. **Be truthful no matter the circumstances**
9. **Have hope**
10. **Do everything that lead to PEACE.**
11. **Make Christ your friend.**

THINGS THAT HINDER PEACE

1. Oneself
2. Denying the faith
3. Loss of hope
4. Satan

5. **Troubles and circumstances**
6. **Unrighteousness**
7. **Distancing oneself from the word of God**
8. **Unable to pray consistency**

NOTE THE FOLLOWING

1. **It is impossible to have PEACE outside God.**
2. **It is impossible to be in Christ without PEACE.**

3. It is impossible to have joy, when you don’t have PEACE.
4. This PEACE surpasses all other peace
5. If you distance yourself from the word of God, then you distance

yourself from this PEACE.

6. PEACE makes one a principal.
7. PEACE removes the hardness of the face.

REMEMBER TO ACCEPT CHRIST JESUS TO BE ABLE TO HAVE PEACE WITH GOD AND THE WORLD.

PEACE OF GOD is non-negotiable.

BY: A.S. PAUL

www.ingramcontent.com/pod-product-compliance
Lightning Source LLC
La Vergne TN
LVHW010506160826
845677LV00012B/2682